# A Woman with
## a Mind of her Own

## Books by Alan R. Tripp

*Millions from the Mind*

*In the Hole!*

*Who Needs Hallmark?*

# A Woman with a Mind of her Own

The Delicious Adventures of Maggie,
Who Lived by Her Own Rules as Daughter,
Wife, Mother, Businesswoman,
Professor, Author, Public Speaker
…and True Feminist

Alan R. Tripp

ARCHWAY
PUBLISHING

Archway Publishing books may be ordered through booksellers or by contacting:

Archway Publishing
1663 Liberty Drive
Bloomington, IN 47403
www.archwaypublishing.com
1 (888) 242-5904

ISBN: 978-1-4808-1617-6 (sc)
ISBN: 978-1-4808-1616-9 (hc)
ISBN: 978-1-4808-1618-3 (e)

Library of Congress Control Number: 2015904784

Print information available on the last page.

Archway Publishing rev. date: 4/6/2015

# Acknowledgements

My gratitude goes to Mary Graff, veteran newspaper editor, for casting her keen eye on both the grammar and the content of this book.

To Layli Marparyan and Barbara Hayes at the Wellesley Centers for Women, and their staff, I offer great appreciation for providing the quoted speech excerpts and other tidbits from *The Maggie Tripp Library.*

And, equally, I thank the consistently professional team at Archway Publishing for moving "A WOMAN" from my computer to the printed page.

# Where to Find It

# But First, This Message …

Many men marry women without really knowing very much about them.

I certainly didn't know Maggie well when we eloped on April 9, 1941, just nine months before the start of World War II. How little I knew is summed up by what her mother's friends were gossiping about at our second wedding: "It'll never last. Wait until he finds out how she behaves!"

Of course I didn't hear about that judgment until years later when Maggie mentioned it to me passingly on our seventieth anniversary.

We were, I should add, married three times: first, we eloped, then we were wed in a double ceremony with Maggie's sister, and, for our twenty-fifth anniversary, we renewed our vows with a written contract to assure the world we would never divorce.

What Maggie did, and the way she did things, made people love her—even though she was always "in charge." How Maggie ran her world is best understood by these true stories and by words she wrote or spoke. Maggie managed not only her own life but often the lives of others, always operating "according to me."

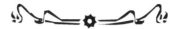

So this is not a conventional biography—you know, a litany of her accomplishments. Rather, it's pointillism with a pen, a mosaic, a collection of character-revealing vignettes to help you peek into her unusual mind through the prism of her escapades.

Because Maggie's ideas about the roles and rights of women permeated everything she did, I have sprinkled direct quotes from her speeches and writings throughout this book.

Maggie Tripp was my wife for seventy-three years. We were so different, nobody could believe we belonged together, but of course that is precisely why it worked so well. That is why I was able to love her deeply and observe her dispassionately.

As you read these vignettes about Maggie, I hope you will be intrigued, fascinated, jealous, enlightened, in awe, tickled, astonished, educated, occasionally aggravated, and, *de minimis,* entertained.

Alan R. Tripp
January 15, 2015

# Baedeker for Maggie's Moniker

Truth be told, Maggie was not her legal name.

In fact, it wasn't even a name of her own choosing.

Over the years, "Maggie" had many names, most of which she adopted herself, names that seemed to fit the occasion, her then current preoccupation, or simply a device to start a new phase of life.

As a consequence of this cognomen rotation, Maggie appears in various vignettes in this book under a variety of identifications—and, in fairness to you, dear readers, here are a few clues as to the names under which she flew through her adventures.

On her birth certificate, her name was Madeline—yes, spelled that way and not Madeleine, as the French would have it. She owed that to her mother, who insisted the simpler spelling was not only correct but would save endless explanations to non-French- speaking Americans.

When she was old enough to write her name, our girl decided on a different spelling, one that would distinguish her from all other Madeleines. She chose Madelyn. Today of course, twisting and mangling the spelling of any name is practically mandatory; back in 1930, it simply foreshadowed other rebellions to come.

About that time, however, Maggie's parents—great movie fans because her father sold candy in theaters—became enamored of the name Madge, a given name shared by movie stars such as Madge Evans and Madge Bellamy. Her parents hung it on their younger daughter, and it remained the name she responded to until the early years of our marriage.

But "Madge" does not have the ring of young love. Try saying it out loud a few times. So when our children began to mouth words, it came out as "Match." Unmatchable, maybe, but not "Match." One day I blurted out Madge Muffin, which clung for a while until Maggie began messing around with my name and Alan became Alley Cat and that became Alley Cott, obviously requiring her to become Magic Cott—which morphed into Magicott, or simply M. Cott. These and other variations flowed freely through our house, but none hung in to become a permanent nickname.

In my more romantic moments, I would call her "Me-Own" or "Lamb Chop" or "Puss Lamb." Sadly, those affectionate appellations never caught on with the kids or her friends. In retrospect, I can see why.

When granddaughter Abby came along, she did what only adorable children, age two, can do: she garbled Grammy into "Ummy"—and it stuck with both family and friends. One of our good friends, upon hearing Ummy for the first time, asked Maggie what corresponding name had been awarded to me; she promptly made up "Pulty." That was an instant winner. Abby adopted it as though it had originated on her lips.

Which brings us to Maggie. In the 1960s, as you will learn elsewhere in this book, Maggie owned an art gallery in Philadelphia, a gallery devoted to exhibiting the work of young, upcoming local artists. Many of these aspiring Warhols, appreciative of the opportunity to be seen in the highly competitive world of contemporary art, became her acolytes.

One day, when munching sandwiches in the gallery, there was sudden silence. One of the artists cleared his throat and said, "You know, we really love having our work in your gallery, but—"

"But what?" she quickly responded.

"Well, we were talking about your name … Madge … it's kind of stuffy, you know, old fashioned … you know, it's kind of harsh for a modern gallery owner."

"So what would you like to call me?"

"We talked it over and we like Maggie."

"So call me Maggie."

From that moment on, they did. And soon the rest of her world did too.

# Managing Mother

**Maggie's** mother, Helen, who at age eighty-five was as outspoken as her daughter, laid her thoughts out for Maggie one day in 1978, essentially like this: "I know you're involved in all that women's-movement stuff. But I just can't understand what you could have to say that people would pay you five thousand dollars to hear you talk for an hour."

No slouch at addressing matters directly, Maggie replied, "The next time I have an engagement, you can go with me, and then you can tell me exactly what you think."

Soon thereafter, Maggie, then living in her elegant apartment at the United Nations Plaza in New York, called her mother in Philadelphia and invited her to come to Pittsburgh, where Maggie would be addressing the Pennsylvania Federation of Women's Clubs. Helen took a plane from Philadelphia while Maggie flew to Pittsburgh from New York. She met her mother at the airport, and they went directly to their room at the Pittsburgh Hilton.

Not one to sit idly by, Helen immediately demanded they go meet the women attending the meeting. But Maggie remembered that I had always cautioned her not to dilute the message by mingling with the crowd before the speech. Afterward, yes, mingle and mix. Before the speech, never.

Instead, Maggie convinced her mother to go down to the auditorium to scout the room, test the microphone, and make sure she would be heard in the farthest corner. It was a very large auditorium indeed, so Maggie parked her mom in the back of the room. She turned on a few stage lights and addressed her one-person audience from the podium.

The title of the speech was "Oh Those Revolutionary Women!" It was a tale of those heroic women, like Mary McCauley ("Molly Pitcher") and Abigail Adams, who had found their own pathways to greatness from the time of the American Revolution until that very day.

After Maggie delivered the first few paragraphs of the speech with gusto, she paused and shouted to Helen, "Well, what do you think?"

From the dark reaches of the auditorium, a voice floated back: "I wish you were two inches taller!"

After the speech, Maggie and Helen joined the women educators for lunch, and the compliments flew thick and fast. Helen glowed.

At the airport, Helen went up the steps to her Philadelphia-bound plane and stopped at the plane entrance. Holding up the entire line of passengers, she turned to Maggie and yelled, "We did all right in Pittsburgh, kid!"

# Oh, Those Revolutionary Women!

Revolution is a good old-fashioned American idea.

We tend to think of the American Revolution as belonging to George Washington, Benjamin Franklin, Thomas Jefferson, and such—strictly a man's affair, except, perhaps, for a little flag sewing done by Betsy Ross.

But there were women in the American Revolution, and there were women fighting for freedom during the entire two hundred years of our Republic.

I call this continuing struggle for equality The Second American Revolution, the one that says women are entitled to all the rights and privileges of human beings in a free land. We're proud to be women and, in some ways, different from men, but unwilling to permit the differences be used as an excuse for restricting our freedom.

—From the "Oh Those Revolutionary Women!" speech before the Pennsylvania Federation of Women's Clubs, 1978

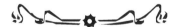

# The Accidental Feminist

Maggie was not born a feminist. She became one only because she did not take offense at the cold stares she received from a group of real feminists when she enrolled at the New School for Social Research in New York City.

The year was 1967. We had just moved to New York because Maggie had grown weary of commuting up and down the Jersey Turnpike from our home in Philadelphia. It required less than a week in New York for Maggie to decide that the Big City could be just as boring as Philadelphia if you didn't do something about it. Several true New Yorkers told her to go to the New School for Social Research down on Thirteenth Street in Greenwich Village, which was then a ragtag neighborhood.

Dressed impeccably in her Peck and Peck suit—perfect for a woman applying for a job in a big New York corporation—Maggie took a taxicab from the United Nations Plaza apartments to the New School. There she charged into the office of the registrar. When the registration clerk asked, "What class are you interested in?" Maggie replied, "Where's the action?"

"Well," said the clerk, "there is a new class forming on the role of women in society. You might like that."

Without hesitation, Maggie signed up and headed directly for the classroom. She did not expect what greeted her. Seated in a lopsided circle was a group of women of various shapes and colors, uniformly dressed in blue jeans. The women turned and stared open-eyed and open-mouthed at their obviously old-school classmate.

Maggie, undaunted, flashed her trademark smile and took a step forward. One of the women motioned her to an adjacent chair.

The outcome was predictable—and all Maggie. In six weeks, she too was dressed in jeans and leading class discussions. And it was at the New School that Maggie met many of the outstanding women, including Gloria Steinem, who later contributed chapters to her 1974 book, *Woman in the Year 2000.*

# Woman in the Year 2000

It's been a long time coming.

Time and again in the course of history, women's voices were raised to demand control over their own lives. Women asked for a voice in the choice of their husbands, their work, their government.

For several thousand years, women's progress was much like the frog in the well: two leaps upward and one back down.

In ancient Egypt, women entered the banking profession, became moneylenders, speculators, and heads of business. By the time of the Roman empire, they were back to lobbying against laws that restricted the amount of gold they could possess, and on the walls of ancient Pompeii, archaeologists found graffiti demanding an equal say in the government for women.

So it went over the centuries. A Charlotte Brontë could write in Jane Eyre: "Women need the same opportunity as man to use their brains and then should not be confined to making pudding or knitting stockings." And men would reply in chorus: "God created women to take care of men and children."

–from *Woman in the Year 2000*
Edited by Maggie Tripp
Published by Arbor House, 1974

# The Maine Way

One summer back in the 1950s, Maggie and her niece Sandy spent the lazy days in side-by-side houses on Long Lake in Maine. When an invitation came from Mike Rogers to visit Camp Tapawingo some twenty-five miles away, they jumped into the car and followed Mike's directions: "Go straight through Bridgton across the causeway at Moose Pond and take the next half-right onto Sweden Road. Just keep going until you see a sign for Camp Tapawingo."

The two women arrived at the camp without missing a turn. Mike had arranged a full day of tennis and swimming, followed by a typical self-service camp dinner, complete with camp songs.

By seven o'clock they were exhausted, quite ready to leave. As they pulled away, Mike shouted, "Just go back the way you came!"

The sun was peeking in and out from behind the hills with flickering, intermittent streaks of bright light and deep shadows across the road. Small doubts began to creep into their minds. The road looked unfamiliar, and they didn't spot any landmarks, country churches or schools, or road signs.

"I think we missed a turn," Maggie said.

"Well, it didn't seem to take so long coming over," Sandy rejoined. "Should we go back?"

At that moment a small truck came down the road toward them. Maggie moved the car to the middle of the road and flashed her lights. The truck stopped.

Maggie said, "Get out and ask him if we're still on the Sweden Road."

Dutifully, Sandy approached the driver with a friendly, "Hi! Thanks for stopping. Are we on the Sweden Road? We're trying to get home to Bridgton."

"Ayuh," the driver answered. "It's the Sweden Road the way I'm goin', but the way you're goin', we call it the Bridgton Road. Got it?"

Maggie and Sandy reached home quickly and safely because, years before GPS was invented, there were simple directions called The Maine Way.

# Women, Women Everywhere

Abigail Adams wrote to her husband, John, then a member of the Continental Congress, "In the new codes and laws which I suppose it will be necessary for you to make, I desire that you would remember the ladies and be more generous and favorable to them than your ancestors …

"If particular care and attention is not paid to the ladies, we are determined to foment a rebellion and will not find ourselves bound by any laws in which we have no voice or representation."

Unfortunately, John Adams was a stick-in-the-mud. He wrote back that he had no intention of being subjected to "the despotism of the petticoat."

The women of today have a new message for Mr. Adams: "Dear John. Don't bother your pretty little head about what men can do for women—we're making the changes for ourselves!"

—from Maggie's lecture "Women, Women Everywhere" at Saint Francis College
Biddeford, Maine
April 1978

# And How Did You Two Meet?

**Numerous** keen-minded people, soon after meeting Maggie and me and noting the striking difference in our outlook and character, would blurt out: "And how did you two meet?" It was a fair question, but the answer was complicated.

The year was 1940. I was working in Camden, New Jersey, for RCA, although I still considered myself a New Yorker and fled back there on weekends. Unbeknownst to me, my mother was playing bridge one day at her apartment in New York where she entertained a woman from Philadelphia. Between hands, Mom mentioned to this woman that her son was single and working near Philadelphia in the dull and dirty city of Camden.

As reported to me later, the Philadelphia lady at once responded with the well-known phrase, "Have I got a girl for him!"

That very night, Mother called me and instructed me to call that Philadelphia lady who would arrange a proper introduction to this wonderful, highly recommended girl.

I called the lady as instructed, and she gushed, "Oh, of course! Of course! Her name is Madge Beresin. I'm sure you'll like her, but I'm packing right now because we're going to France for three weeks. Now, hold on—I'll call her mother and explain who you are, and she'll tell her daughter that you will call. When I return, I'll arrange to introduce you more formally, but I know you don't want to wait for three weeks."

Yes, I almost always did what my mother told me to do. I called Madge, we dated, we fell in love—and in three months, we had a fight and split. I still hadn't met the lady who "introduced" us.

By the following summer, Camden was becoming oppressive. Between the summer heat, the aroma of tomatoes from the Campbell's soup factory, and the flecks of sawdust in the air from the RCA radio cabinet factory, I felt a desperate urge to get out.

Perhaps that girl wasn't so bad after all. Perhaps I should call Madge and make up.

But Madge didn't answer the phone—her mother did. "Well, Alan," Mrs. Beresin said. "Madge isn't here. She's taking summer classes at the University of Wisconsin, but I'm sure she'll be very, very glad to hear from you. As a matter of fact, she's coming home next week. Why don't you surprise her and meet her at the airport? I have the flight number right here."

And that is how, late afternoon of the next Tuesday, I found myself at the Philadelphia airport eagerly awaiting this girl who had grown more and more beautiful in my imagination.

There only one difficulty—never telling her mother Madge had invited her then boyfriend to meet her at the plane. He won the tossup for taking her home, but I won the war, and within a few months, she kissed him good-bye.

I finally met the lady from Philadelphia at our wedding … where she apologized for never having properly introduced us.

There is a back story that Madge never told me until several years after we were married. The day after she had agreed on the telephone to have a "blind date" with me, she got cold feet.

*Who was this guy from New York? What did anybody really know about him? Why had her mother agreed without even knowing him? Was he short, was he ugly, was he dumb?*

In her typical "if you don't like it, change it" fashion, she turned to her sister, Ruth, and said, "Look, Ruth, I have all this homework to do. I simply can't take the time to go out with this guy. Why don't you go instead? Just tell him your name is Madge and he won't know the difference. Spend one evening with him and lose the bum. Listen, I'll give you five bucks if you do this for me."

To Ruth's everlasting credit, she flatly refused. And as a result, I was stuck with Madge for seventy-three years.

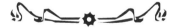

# The Free Married Woman

There is hope for marriage.

A short twenty-five years ago such a statement would have seemed obvious. Today the problems inherent in conventional marriage are discussed at dinners and in magazines, documented in statistical reports and flashed across the television screen. This is not significant merely in the abstract; this is happening to your friends or parents or to your children or perhaps to you.

A number of solutions are being suggested: group marriage. "Term marriage." Ménage à trois. Permanent singleness.

Amidst all the uproar, almost no one has noticed that one party to the marriage contract is changing many of the provisions of the agreement. With the reawakening of women's consciousness about themselves as individual human beings rather than as vestigial appendages of males, millions of American women will, during the next twenty-five years, be creating an entirely new kind of marriage.

The marriage ritual will remain. But the relationship within the marriage will be sharply altered. The new marriage may look similar to the old marriage on the outside, but new attitudes and a mature sense of self from the female partner will create a different kind of give-and-take between married men and women.

The American male has always thought of himself as free … until he was married. The new American woman is about to show him that freedom is indivisible, that a marriage in which both partners are free and un-dependent is the only kind you can live with over time.

–From "The Free Married Woman" in *Woman in the Year 2000*
Published by Arbor House, 1974

# School Days, School Days

When Maggie was in high school, she found a simple way to become a popular president of the class. She ran for office by promising there would be less homework and more extracurricular activities.

To deliver on this promise—like a lot of political promises—would be impossible. But Maggie had anticipated the problem. During the election, she had promised nine different classmates that she would appoint them as vice president.

And that's what she did. She appointed a vice president for each target—more gym time, late-arrival forgiveness, prom planning, etc.—all things promised during the campaign. The result was that the nine vice presidents did all the work, and each one appointed a subcommittee. It was like a pyramid scheme with half the class having a non-paying job in Maggie's administration.

This arrangement gave President Maggie the notion that it was all right to talk during class, flirt with the boys, or cut out in the afternoon for a movie. She tested all the rules and conquered all the tests.

In those days, however, each student had to bring his or her report card home and have a parent sign it, acknowledging parental awareness of that child's school record.

Grading in Maggie's class was based on three things: effort, conduct, and (academic) performance. Maggie's report card consistently read P-P-9. Decoded, this meant poor for effort and poor for conduct, but a nine out of ten for performance, close to the best academic grade possible.

School days surely presaged Maggie's talent for breaking the rules without being tagged as just plain bad.

# Managing by Instinct

**Books** and books have been written about "how to manage people." Maggie knew how to manage people without ever reading one line on the subject. She did it by sheer instinct.

Many of the vignettes recounted here illustrate this native sense that permitted her to have her way while convincing the other person, either willingly or helplessly, to accept the verdict.

In her teen years as "Madge," no one was a greater challenge than her father, Jack. Here was a man who exuded warmth and radiated success. In his own business world—selling popcorn and candy in theaters—he managed to own the right to sell such goodies in the majority of the motion-picture houses in the United States. And he did it with a unique combination of charm and acumen, the kind of charm that convinced each person he or she was the only one in the world he wanted to meet that day, the kind of acumen that turned him into an uncharted bank.

You might imagine that such a man would have little difficulty controlling a mere teenage girl. Normally, yes. "Madgically," no way. One example will do.

When Madge was in her teenage years, her father imposed a curfew on Saturday night dates: midnight. To Madge this was not a fixed number but rather a challenge. After several skirmishes with her father had ended in brief groundings, she discovered a simple way to violate the curfew—one that did not fool her father but left him feeling satisfied that he was still in charge.

Upon hearing the apartment door open and shut, Jack would bellow from his bedroom, "Madge, what time is it?" Knowing full well that it was close to one in the morning, she would respond, "It's plenty after eleven." And she learned to enunciate the word "plenty" so that it was largely indistinguishable from "twenty."

Thus the power struggle ended in a tie. Jack was satisfied that his daughter knew he was monitoring her behavior. And, instinctively, Madge had found a way to get her way with her father.

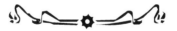

## A Feminist Talks to Retailers

I'm happy to see that so many of you showed up for what the press usually calls "A Woman's Libber." I don't know what you'll call me by the end of this meeting, but I hope you'll call me "A Retailer's Best Friend."

When I told my husband I was going to talk about the Women's Movement to people who represent some of the best department stores in America, I asked him what I could say at the outset that would make everyone feel relaxed. He suggested I should call this speech, "A sure-fire method for beating last year's figures, month by month!"

–From "A Feminist Talks to Retailers"
National Retail Merchants Association
January 1973

# Runaway

**Maggie** did not have to become a rebel; she was born one.

While I have no concrete evidence of her childhood behavior, I do have, from her own lips, a tale of rebellion that would give many parents the shakes.

At ten years of age, after four years of camp experience, starting out as "Baby Woodmere," Maggie's parents, in their wisdom, sent her to a new summer camp—without consulting her. Upon arrival, Maggie quickly determined that she did not like the counselor, that the kids in her bunk were nerds, that it would rain every day, and that her bed was extremely uncomfortable.

Of course many children have experienced dismay on one level or another at summer camp. (I refer you to Alan Sherman's famous recording, "Hello Muddah, Hello Faddah … here I am at Camp Granada.")

But as Maggie many years later reported it to me, she had no patience for an exchange of letters with her parents or for a fruitless discussion with the camp director. Instead, she packed a few clothes in a small bag, leaving her camp trunk behind, and walked a mile to the nearest small town where she boarded a bus for Philadelphia. At the first bus stop, she found a pay phone and placed a collect call to her home and announced to her shocked mother that she would arrive in Philadelphia in two hours and would her mom please meet her at the bus station.

The camp director was furious, having spent a full day searching for a missing camper. Maggie's mother wouldn't talk to her for two days. Maggie's father reprimanded her, but only mildly. She suspected he actually admired her guts.

In any event, Maggie certainly had set a precedent for her later dramatic exit from Barnard College. (See the next story.)

# Love It or Leave It

Rebellion in college manifests itself in many interesting ways. Some students simply write angry letters to their parents. Others join causes and march across the campus.

None of the obvious rebellions suited Maggie. Instead, she simply packed up and left the college where her father had exerted great effort to secure her admission.

When Maggie finished her senior year at Overbrook High School in Philadelphia—consistently scoring at the top of her class—she assumed every college would welcome her with open arms. She wanted to go to one of the "seven sisters" colleges, but her father insisted she stay close to home. After much jousting, her dad agreed she could go as far as Barnard College in New York.

Upon applying to Barnard, Maggie was shocked to find that the New York State Regents Examination was a requirement. Oh well! What was one more examination?

It turned out that both the format and the content of the Regents exam was totally different from anything taught in Philadelphia. Maggie's score would never get her into Barnard. But of course Daddy would not let his darling daughter be defeated by a quirk of the education system. Jack telephoned Bob Christenberry, the general manager of the Astor Hotel in New York, but far more than that, a political power in the Big City—and, miracle of miracles, Maggie was admitted to Barnard College.

Maggie found Barnard quite the opposite of all her teenage expectations of joy and excitement in college. She was assigned to a six by nine room furnished with a bed, bureau, desk, and some coat racks. There was a community bathroom down the hall. But worst of all, there was a long set of rules posted on the back of the door:

*Return to your room by ten o'clock.*

*Lights out by eleven.*

*Only textbooks are permitted in your room.*

*The gates to the campus separating Barnard and Columbia will be locked promptly at nine p.m.*

It took Maggie just five weeks of internal fury to reach her boiling point. She asked for an appointment with the dean, Virginia Gildersleeve.

She told the dean that the college was boring and uninspiring and added, "Dean Gildersleeve, I think you just don't understand male-female relationships."

Dean Gildersleeve was understandably apoplectic. "You're a very brash young woman," she told Maggie. "If you don't like it here, you can resign."

Maggie paused only briefly and said, "I do."

Maggie's mother's response to her daughter's return was "Humph!"

Maggie's father simply said, "Well, what now?"

"I'm going back to Penn where most of my friends are anyway. I'll go to summer school to make up the credits and graduate without losing a term."

And that's how Maggie managed to graduate from the University of Pennsylvania in 1942 along with many of her friends – by making up the credits lost at Barnard with two lovely summer school sessions, one at Cornell, one in Wisconsin.

There's a coda to this story.

Some thirty years later, when Maggie had become the resident maven of women's studies at The New School, she was invited to be the principal speaker at a Barnard program on women's new roles. She opened her talk with a confession of her prior six weeks at Barnard. Then she pointed up to the heavens and said, "Virginia Gildersleeve—wherever you are—as I told you way back then, you just didn't understand male-female relationships."

The crowd roared appreciation for Maggie's insight to their late Dean.

# The Future World of Work for Women

Intellectually, men—especially young men—seem to accept the new roles of women. In a ten-year study of students at six hundred colleges, two-thirds of freshmen in 1967 agreed with this statement: "The activities of married women are best confined to home and the family." By 1976, fewer than 30 percent agreed with that. And today I'm sure the percentage is much less.

Some men see women as job competition—which they well may be. Some have found themselves with a female boss. Men are learning behavior adjustments when a businesswoman picks up the check or when a traveling associate is female.

*Newsweek* reported a Northwestern University senior who said: "I'm in the first generation to grow up with feminism. We'll be the first to take it full cycle. But who needs the pressure of being a typical male? It's more fun being a human first."

—From the speech "The Future World of Work for Women—and What It Means to Men"
Eastern Michigan University
February 1979

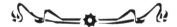

# Corrupting Carol

To be extremely popular with your nieces, it is generally necessary to avoid acting as their mother. Maggie knew this very well, perhaps reinforced by the fact that her sister was a well-behaved model mother, and her two nieces, Sandy and Carol, were brought up to behave as young ladies from day one.

As a result, when Carol, the younger girl, came to visit Maggie at our rented boathouse in Maine, she eagerly looked forward to exploring entirely new worlds with her wild "Auntie Maine," as they dubbed her.

"When can we start drinking?" Carol asked shortly after her arrival.

"Have you ever tasted alcohol?" Maggie responded.

"No," Carol said. "That's part of my Maine adventure. That's why I came to see you."

"The first thing you have to know is that you don't start drinking until dark—until the sun is over the yardarm. Otherwise you may find yourself starting at lunch and continuing right through dinner. That's how people become alcoholics."

Since it was midsummer, the sun did not disappear until well after seven o'clock. At that point, Maggie carefully prepared two vodka-and-tonics, and, with a warning to "just sip," she launched her niece into the pleasures of a pre-dinner drink. It turned out Carol's chemistry handled liquor very well and her social career was launched.

The next day, as late afternoon approached, a storm came roaring in. As the dark clouds covered the sky and the ripples on the lake showed whitecaps, Carol turned to her Auntie Maine and said, "Gee, it's getting pretty dark. Can we start drinking now?"

Maggie proceeded to explain, tongue-in-cheek, that linking your drinking to the weather is another booby trap for drunkards.

Carol obviously was a good student and always maintained a nice balance between pre-dinner cocktails and postprandial behavior.

# Of Course I Can Cook That!

As Maggie grew from girlhood to womanhood, she successfully escaped any exposure to cooking. At home, her mother ran the kitchen—planned the menus, ordered the groceries, did the cooking. Maggie skipped home economics at school—and at home.

Her sister, Ruth, always Maggie's opposite, would hang about the kitchen, learning to cook by observation, occasionally as sous chef. Maggie did her homework or hung out with school friends until 5:55 p.m., leaving a five-minute window to wash up and take her place at the table.

In our first year of marriage, Maggie was still in college, and I was promoting big-band records for RCA. So dinner was catch-as-catch-can. But in a first year together, food isn't always the first thing on your mind.

During my four years of military service during World War II, I was assigned briefly to Ft. Monmouth, New Jersey, where I promptly rented an off-post apartment where Maggie and I could share a bit of domesticity and avoid eating army food.

Thanksgiving rolled around, and Maggie said we ought to have a traditional dinner at home. I ordered the turkey from the army PX, where the price was right, and asked if I could invite one or two of my less-fortunate fellow officers (all bachelors) to this stellar occasion.

On the designated day, Maggie and I drove to the PX. I went in and bought the bird, which was already bagged with my name plainly written on the package; I returned to the car and proudly handed the turkey to my spouse.

By the time I walked around the car and opened the door, Maggie was screaming, "Oh, no! No, no, no! You can't be serious!"

There, on the seat, lay my purchase, the bag torn half-open, the turkey's head and feathered body revealed. It was dead all right—dead but nothing more.

"Drive," she said. "Drive me to the A&P."

Maggie carried the bird into the market while I sat quietly observing her through the store window.

She placed the turkey on the meat counter and leaned over to talk to the butcher. I could imagine the conversation: "You can't believe what my dumb husband did. He bought this turkey at the army PX and never asked them to clean it. What can you expect of a second lieutenant? Can you help me—please!"

The butcher lifted the bird from the counter and turned to his chopping block.

Ten minutes later, Maggie emerged from the A&P, a smile on her face, the bird in hand. "He didn't even charge me for doing it," she said, sprinkling salt on my wounded ego.

That evening about eight o'clock, as I sat in the living room reading a book, I noticed Maggie had left the room. I traced her to the kitchen. There, sitting on a kitchen stool before the open-doored refrigerator, sat Maggie, her hand under her chin, elbow on her leg, staring intently into the box—at the turkey. On her lap was a cookbook.

"What in the world are you doing?" I asked.

"I'm figuring out how to cook this thing. I never cooked a turkey before."

By six o'clock the next morning, Maggie was in the kitchen. With a little help from a willing assistant (me), dinner was served at one in the afternoon, eliciting the highest praise from one of our guests: "It's as good as my mom's!"

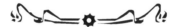

# Portrait of a New Woman—The Fine Art of Change

*One thing has irrevocably changed: the image* women have of themselves.

There is a new woman out there. She is no longer two-dimensional or a soft-focus Impressionist figure. She is Cubist in her many roles—lover, athlete, politician, educator, moneymaker, president, and mother. More and more, this new woman represents social realism, often painted in the school of super-realism. She is willing to search for the meaning in abstract Expressionism.

Art reflects life, and life mirrors art. Today's woman is not just the subject for paintings but the creator of art, both on canvas and in fresh lifestyles. I think we're looking good, don't you?

—From "Portrait of a New Woman—the Fine Art of Change"
International Federation of Teachers
Ottawa, Canada, July 1980

# The Wide World of Art

While Maggie was busy gaining admission to Wharton business classes at Penn, she also found time to take graduate classes in fine art with famed art critic and professor Dr. John McCoubrey. The combination, she thought, equipped her to become an owner of an art gallery in downtown Philadelphia.

Together with partner Teddy Jacobs, she opened Gallery 252 at that address on South Sixteenth Street in downtown Philadelphia. To crash a well-saturated market, they featured only young contemporary artists. It was a thing of beauty. The walls were overflowing with oil paintings, collages, watercolors, and pen-and-ink sketches.

On opening day, dressed in a charming black suit with a small gold pin on the lapel, Maggie sat behind the small desk at the rear of the gallery.

Suddenly the front door opened and a man entered. He was dressed in overalls with a rolled-up paper object under his arm. "You sell paintin's?" he asked.

Maggie rose from her chair and, fairly oozing charm, said, "Of course, young man, come right in. What did you have in mind?"

"You seem like a very nice lady," the young man offered, "so I'll tell you the story. You see, I've got this girl I'm livin' with in an apartment on Third Street, and she asked me to wallpaper the livin' room. I did a real good job exceptin' I have a space about two by three feet with not enough wallpaper to cover it up. So I said I would buy her a paintin' to go in that space. That's why I brought this sample of the wallpaper—so you could see the color and give me something to match."

After a thorough study of the paintings in the gallery, Maggie was still unable to provide the exact solution to his problem. Then it occurred to her that this gentlemen might have a limited budget. "How much did you have in mind spending for this painting?"

"I've got fifty bucks left from the wallpaper. I'll blow the whole thing if I can get the right paintin'."

"Well you really don't want an oil painting. You need a print—and we have two bins of them in the back room."

As she walked back to the storeroom, a thought occurred to her: *Oh my God! I'm taking this guy back into the dark store-room, and he's going to rape me.*

In fact, the young man did no such thing but rather helped her lift and shift bins of sketches until they found one by Edna Gass, a nice woodsy scene that picked up some of the tone of the wallpaper.

"That's perfect," the customer said. "How much do I owe you?"

"That'll be $47.75, including tax. Let me wrap it for you."

"Nah. I'll just put it inside the wallpaper. Here's my fifty bucks. And lady, you've been awfully nice—so just keep the change."

It was the first and last time Maggie ever received a tip.

# Legal Tender Has No Gender

I think it's pretty wonderful that we are having a symposium on planning for financial independence here at Wellesley. Not at Harvard or Yale or Brown—not at Penn, my alma mater, or at The New School for Social Research where I teach—but at Wellesley, a stout advocate of independent education for women. And by the way, did you notice that I'm the only outside speaker here who is a woman?

Dr. Kenneth Galbraith wrote in his book titled *Money*, "Most things in life—automobiles, mistresses, cancer—are important only to those who have them. Money, in contrast, is equally important to those who have it and those who don't." I hope that explains to your satisfaction why this talk on budgeting is titled "Legal Tender Has No Gender."

—From "Legal Tender Has No Gender"
Symposium at Wellesley College
Spring 1976

# Speaking One's Mind

As noted elsewhere in this book, Maggie could manage anybody at any time—well almost. Managing her mother was done pretty much after the damage was done.

During our early years in New York City, *New York* magazine did a feature story on seven couples that were not only married but were enjoying two careers. The title was "He Works, She Works, but How Does the House Work?"

At that point in history, the very idea of a man and woman both having successful careers, each going his or her own way in the daytime yet snuggling up at night was clearly challenging to pedestrian minds. Shortly after the article appeared we received a call from the producers of the television show *Not for Women Only*. Would we be willing to tell our story to Frank Field and Polly Bergen?

Would we! Not only did we inform our friends, far and wide, but Maggie promptly invited her mother, Helen, to come to New York for the taping of the program.

Maggie met her mother at Penn Station and taxied her up to the sixty-eighth street studios. Before retreating backstage to join me in makeup, she found a seat for her mother in the front row of the audience.

*Not For Women Only* was being taped for later airing, market by market. The house lights were dimmed, and the announcer intoned: "From New York City, we bring you *Not For Women Only*, starring Frank Field and Polly Bergen. And for our first guests, here is that super couple, Maggie and Alan Tripp!"

In a split second, a voice rose from the audience, bellowing, "What's so super about them?"

"*Cut!*" a filtered voice from the control room screamed. The recording session was halted; the lights went up.

Ushers quickly searched the audience for the source of that challenging question. But Maggie had no doubt. She knew the voice. She knew the tone, and she knew the source of that shattering enquiry. She rushed down to the audience, sat her mother down, and reassured the assistant director there would never, ever in her lifetime be a recurrence of her mother's audience participation.

And there wasn't. Of course that didn't stop Helen from telling the story to her friends back in Philadelphia.

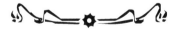

# Making Money Work is Woman's Work

There was a time, not too long ago, when the only thing most women knew about money was how to spend it. And how much she spent depended on how well she manipulated her man.

I remember a play called *Life with Father*, in which Mother buys a new lamp for the house. When Father complains about the purchase, she says, "But it didn't cost anything, dear. I already had a credit at the store for the hat you made me return!"

I'm not convinced Mother was so dumb in dealing with Father. But I'm quite sure she didn't know how to deal with money ... acquire it, manage it, control it. Well, times change—and today's woman knows that money has no secondary sex characteristics.

—From the seminar "Making Money Work Is Woman's Work Now"
Merrill Lynch
Austin, Texas, February 1978

# A Dog's Life

They say a dog is man's best friend. On the other hand, Maggie provided evidence that a woman can be a dog's best friend.

In our days of enjoying our newly built house in Rydal, Pennsylvania, we added a magnificent, full-blooded Airedale dog to the household. We named him Fitzgerald.

Fitz was tall and strong—and stubborn. But how we loved him! He was gentle with the children and rough on everything else. He repeatedly tore up the plant box in the living room, sprinkling dirt for several yards down the new carpeting.

After cleaning up Fitzgerald's mess several times, I spoke to him sternly. I threatened him with banishment and then shunned him for several days. The result of my efforts was that he cleaned out the plant box so thoroughly we needed a professional rug cleaner. I ceded my position as dog trainer to Maggie.

Even under Maggie's watchful eye and commanding voice, Fitzgerald did not quickly lapse into tranquility. As he reached maturity, another interest turned his attention away from the living room. It seems that he was endowed with extraordinary olfactory powers, and when a female dog was in heat anywhere within five miles of our home, Fitzgerald was the first dog to know about it. He repeatedly took off in response to such a signal and followed his nose, wherever it led him. Maggie would have none of this. She called the cops, and the kind police of Abington Township would regularly arrive in our driveway with Fitzgerald sitting up proudly on the backseat of the patrol car.

One day, when Fitzgerald had disappeared for an extraordinarily long time, Maggie saw the police car arrive in our driveway—without our favorite dog in the backseat. A policeman came to the door and sadly informed her that Fitzgerald had been hit by an automobile on Meetinghouse Road, a quarter mile away, and asked if she would come to get him, Quickly throwing on a sweater, Maggie jumped into her car and followed the police.

Meetinghouse Road is a main drag, a two-lane road with shoulders and plenty of traffic. There, blocking one lane, lay Fitzgerald, motionless.

Maggie sat on the road next to her dog, stroked him gently, and whispered, "Fitzgerald, you keep breathing. If you keep breathing, your mother can help you. If you stop breathing, your mother can't help you."

She repeated this mantra for some ten minutes while the police generously directed traffic around her until an animal ambulance appeared and Fitzgerald was carefully carried off to a nearby animal hospital.

Fitzgerald lived.

It required three weeks in the hospital with some wonderful bone setting by the vet. And, to get Fitzgerald back on his feet, it required Maggie's constant visits plus some imagination to restore his appetite. Fitz had refused to eat dog food, even refused his onetime favorite, hamburger. But Maggie persisted until one day, visiting the dog on her way home from a delicatessen, she offered him chopped chicken liver on the tip of her finger. After some ceremonious sniffing, Fitzgerald's tongue came out and cautiously licked the liver. Soon Maggie's entire liver inventory disappeared.

A few weeks after liver restored his appetite, Fitzgerald was back in the house, a slower, wiser, and, quite possibly, a dearer companion.

And he never again tore up the plant box in the living room.

# The Two-Occasion Wedding Dress

In the ongoing lifelong struggle between Maggie and her mother to determine who would manage whom, their joint shopping expeditions were always a hoot. Helen had grown up in a very middle-class family where shopping for a bargain was the only way to shop. Maggie grew up in a family of some substance where admitting you were wealthy was itself a sin.

When the time came for our daughter's wedding, the event was planned for the Helmsley Palace Hotel in New York—actually, not in the hotel itself but in the magnificent Villard Houses, the hundred-year-old townhouses now attached to the hotel.

Helen told Maggie she wanted to be the most elegantly dressed person at the wedding; Maggie, in turn, invited Helen to come to New York to shop on the concierge floor of Saks Fifth Avenue. This floor, as you may know, housed only the great designer couture.

After scanning several of the "exhibits" and listening to the phony flattery that is the stock-in-trade of people selling expensive women's clothing, Helen began to respond with sharp phrases such as "Nonsense!" or "Actually, I hate it!"

Then, Helen saw one dress that caught her fancy. It was silver and gold lamé accented with panels of lace. It sparkled everywhere. She tried it on, and there was no doubt in her mind or Maggie's that it was perfect.

Only one challenge remained: the price.

Helen's frame of reference was Zeldin's, a small discount dress shop in West Philadelphia. Maggie's orientation ranged from Bergdorf Goodman to Saks Fifth Avenue.

Quick as a magician, Maggie grabbed the price tag. The digits read $6,000. When Helen asked her how much the dress cost, Maggie put her finger over the last zero and showed her the tag. Helen exclaimed, "Six hundred dollars! Now that's reasonable. I told you, you never get your pockets picked at Tiffany's!" (Metaphorically speaking.)

The dress was indeed a great sensation at daughter Barbara's wedding. But Helen, ever true to her thrifty roots, was not finished. After the wedding, she told Maggie, "I want to be buried in that dress."

And so she was, making the Saks Fifth Avenue dress a super-bargain at any price.

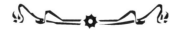

# ERA Debate with Phyllis Schlafly

I've been working on a book called *Money, Love, Children, and Me* ... here are a few words on what's happening between women and men on those four topics.

*Money.* The stereotype is that women only know how to spend money. The fact is, they can make money and manage money. Banks, insurance companies, and colleges are running seminars to teach the financial facts of life. It's a basic step toward marital sanity.

*Love.* Intimacy and companionship are now co-equals with simple emotional feelings. And sexual satisfaction is an essential goal for both the man and the woman.

*Children.* There are still many "supermoms"—women holding a full-time job, running a household, caring for children, and massaging their man's back or ego or both. However, especially among young husbands, there is a new trend toward "fathering." This kind of fathering means spending time with the child that not only permits the mother to do other things but helps educate and mold the child.

*Me.* "Me" covers how you feel about yourself—the personal satisfaction with what you are doing with your life and the nourishment you are getting from the relationship.

—From the ERA debate with Phyllis Schlafly
Wyandot Center, Kansas City, Kansas
October 1979

# Maggie Meets the Presidents

In the course of lobbying for the Equal Rights Amendment, Maggie met not one president but two: Jimmy Carter and Ronald Reagan. In both situations, she was given their full attention and left feeling that she had them on her side. But as we all know, politicians are good at agreeing with you without necessarily agreeing to do what you want.

This was the case with Carter the Democrat and Reagan the Republican.

Maggie met Jimmy Carter when we both went to the White House with a small group representing the businessman's committee for the ERA, which I helped found, and the New School for Social Research, where Maggie was then head of women's studies.

In addition to a lovely reception and dinner, we were given a ten-minute private audience with Carter. He listened very carefully to our case, namely that opening the road to equality for women would help bring the best possible brains to American industry and government. Carter agreed with the principle and very cautiously said he would be on the right side when the issue came to his desk.

The Ronald Reagan encounter was more casual. A major luncheon was held at the Commodore Hotel in New York as part of a national conference on pathways to better business. Reagan was the guest of honor and a speaker.

Representing academia in New York and in her role as the maven of women's studies at the New School, Maggie was invited to the luncheon.

How it happened she never did find out, but Maggie was seated on the dais next to Ronald Reagan. He was charming and attentive. After the introductions, Maggie promptly took the opportunity to make her case for the ERA. Reagan listened intently. He smiled, nodded, and focused solely upon Maggie.

"I was surprised at how receptive Reagan was," Maggie told me later. "I couldn't sit there and take notes, but afterward it was clear to me that he was listening without really hearing what I was saying about the ERA. No wonder he is such a sensational politician—he could make anyone believe he was on their side."

Maggie saw Reagan one more time, in the elevator of our apartment house in New York, the United Nations Plaza. He nodded to her, although she didn't believe he actually remembered her name. But what Maggie remembered was his shirt: "I never saw such a white shirt on a man anywhere. It was pure white. I don't think he has his shirts laundered—I think he just puts a new one on everyday."

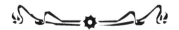

# Letter from Sarah Weddington

Excerpt from Sarah Weddington's letter to Monique Pelletier:

"I have asked Ms. Maggie Tripp to bring you greetings from the United States. President Carter and I are delighted to know that such a broad cross-section of the French populace is interested in what may be one of the greatest social revolutions of the twentieth century, the movement on behalf of women's rights.

"As a new special assistant to the president, I would like especially to extend my greetings and congratulations to Mme. Monique Pelletier, the newly appointed minister delegate for the condition of women in France.

"Again, our best wishes for a most successful conference on a topic of great importance to both our nations."

–Letter written by Sarah Weddington, President Carter's special assistant, to Monique Pelletier, France's first minister for women
October 1978

# An Olympic Mind

If there was a prize in the Olympic games for speed of observation and decision, Maggie would surely have won. Time and again, while the rest of us normal human beings were still musing over a situation, Maggie would deliver the answer. A few simple examples will illuminate this point.

While we were riding through Paris in a taxicab, Maggie suddenly screamed, "Stop! Stop! Tell the driver to pull over!"

Since that command was obviously intended for me, and since I had no idea what tragedy or opportunity had stimulated Maggie's decision, I yelled to the driver, "*Arrêtez! Arrêtez!*"

The driver slammed on the brakes—as did several cars behind us. He swerved to the curb, turned to me, and asked in French if my wife was having a heart attack—or something to that effect. I assured the driver that there was no indication of an immediate calamity and said to Maggie, "You could get us killed like that. What in the world is going on?"

"Didn't you see it? Of course you didn't. We just passed the Bonpoint store. The most beautiful children's clothing in the world. I'm not leaving Paris without getting something for Abby."

The driver, who understood only a little English but picked up immediately on the name Bonpoint, said to me, "*Mais certainment, Monsieur. Ces sont vêtements pour les enfants, les plus belles, mais très chères.*"

Then, with no further word from me, he made a U-turn and delivered us to the door. Maggie swept into Bonpoint and soon emerged with her arms chock-a-block with boxes, enough to dress our two-year-old granddaughter for several years.

The taxi driver recovered his good spirits long enough to drive us safely to our hotel, expecting and getting a good tip.

On another occasion in Paris, as we were strolling down Boulevard Saint-Germain, Maggie suddenly became acutely aware that the Parisian air was something less than pure. In fact, the air was thoroughly laced with the exhaust fumes of a million automobiles and motorcycles, none of which was equipped with the kind of exhaust filters required in the United States. Maggie decided on the spot that this pollution was adversely affecting her skin. As we reached the corner, her eyes fell upon a chemist shop, a very high-class European style drugstore.

"There, Alan—that's the very place. That's where they would know about face creams that would protect women against this Paris air. Now do go in there and talk to them and buy me very best face cream in France!"

"But darling, I don't know any of the French words for cosmetics."

"I know that, dear, but you're a man and you can always tell them you're trying to buy a present for your wife. Everyone loves a man who does nice things for his wife, so they'll pay attention to you."

Maggie was right. After using my limited French to explain my predicament, to ask for help in finding the best face cream for my femme, the young woman in the chemist shop immediately explained to me that RoC made a product exactly for this purpose and she succeeded in relieving me of some two hundred francs.

It was worth it. Maggie admired my valiant effort and loved the cream—so much so that when we returned stateside, she insisted I should find the American distributor for RoC. The product was nowhere to be found. I called the company's headquarters in France and was told to be patient, that their products were so much in demand that American distribution would have to wait. Two years later, RoC was all over American drugstores. The brand had been acquired by Johnson & Johnson.

Maggie's legendary response time deserves one more story.

While teaching at the New School for Social Research, Maggie met—and almost invariably liked—many people who were famous, then or later: author and social activist Letty Cottin Pogrebin, Gloria Steinem, Alvin Toffler, and Lois Gould, to name a few. There were only a few on her "don't like" list; one was Betty Friedan.

After teaching class one day, Maggie was descending in a crowded New School elevator when Friedan entered at a lower floor and muscled her way into the car.

Someone in the front grumbled, "Who do you think you are?"

Friedan said, "Young woman, you'll remember I'm Betty Friedan."

In a split second, from the back of the elevator, a voice stage-whispered, "I forgive you."

That someone, of course, was Maggie.

# Travel Simplified

Whenever we traveled abroad, Maggie insisted on "uncomplicated" arrangements—like first-class seats on a plane or a first-class room in a small hotel. Most of the time she got what she wanted.

In certain cases, however, the facts of life were beyond my control.

When we visited Greece, we found Athens an easy city to navigate on foot. What was not easy were the names of the streets. They were all in Greek, a language that had been omitted from our early education.

Maggie quickly created mnemonics by corrupting the sound of these names. Konstantinoupoleos Avenue became Connie's Avenue. Mitropoleos Street convoluted into Mickey Mouse Street.

Kifissias Street proved to a bit of a challenge. After a short consultation with me, Maggie agreed on the inevitable solution: "Kiss Ass Street."

Our exit from Athens proved to be quite exciting, thanks to Maggie's insistence that we should get the best possible flight back to New York. A few hours at the TWA (Trans-World Airlines, which no longer exists) ticket office proved fruitful. They had just put on a new all-business-class plane that would leave Athens on the exact day we wanted to fly.

On the morning of departure, our taxi arrived at the airport in ample time, the check-in line was short (with a special counter for that flight), and a red carpet was rolled out from the airport door to the stairway up to the plane. As we walked along that carpet, a charming young lady placed a bouquet of roses in Maggie's arms.

It was a beautiful plane, a new Douglas DC-7. The seating was simple: two on the right and two on the left.

Precisely on time, the doors were closed and the stewardess announced: "Welcome to the inaugural TWA flight, nonstop from Athens to New York City. We will be in the air for only fourteen hours. Please tell us if there is anything we can do to make your flight completely comfortable."

Maggie exploded. "Nonstop! Fourteen hours! I can't sit in this seat for fourteen hours. Period. I want to get off right now!"

Most of the people in the seats near us heard her and broke out in laughter. The stewardess—yes, that's what we called them then—came over with glasses of champagne to quell the rebellion.

Maggie, after explaining to me that I should always ask the arrival time of a flight, settled back with a book. Champagne and good food made the flight seem shorter.

# No Good Deed Goes Unpunished

One of the wonderful things about small towns in Maine—certainly including Bridgton, where we lived for several months each year at our summer home, Camp Reveille—is the way folks take care of each other.

In our town, if a family had serious trouble, the townsfolk all pitched in. Many towns do this. The way they did it in Bridgton was revealing of that town's particular culture.

Maggie learned about this with an unusual adventure. She had read an ad in *The Bridgton News* with this headline: Cake Bake for the Benefit of a Certain Person. The details followed, like where to donate your cake or how to bid to buy one. But there was no mention of the beneficiary. None.

Impressed by the ingenuity and the anonymity and tactfulness of this fundraiser, Maggie roused our niece, Sandy, then living in the house next door, declaring that they must at once purchase the ingredients for a No-Fail Chocolate Cake, a recipe Maggie had been saving but never used, in anticipation of some special occasion such as this.

Together Sandy and Maggie charged to the local grocery store for the No-Fail Cake ingredients. Just as they were paying the grocery bill, Maggie remembered she had no baking pan at our vacation house.

"The flea market! Go to the flea market!" Sandy said. "You can get everything there for cheap."

"Right," Maggie answered, "'cause I don't think I'll ever do this again."

They dashed to the local flea market where they readily found a large cake pan, one quite worthy of their pioneering experiment.

Back at Camp Reveille, Maggie and Sandy meticulously mixed the ingredients for the No-Fail Chocolate Cake. They preheated the oven to 350°. They set the stove alarm for forty-five minutes and retired to their rocking chairs on the outside deck to enjoy an afternoon cocktail and calm their nerves by simply gazing at Long Lake.

Half an hour later, Sandy exclaimed, "I think I smell something!" She ran to the kitchen, Maggie close behind. There was their cake spread all over the bottom of the oven, beginning to ooze down to the floor. When the situation had cooled down enough to remove the debris, they analyzed the problem: the cake pan had a small hole in its bottom! In their joy at finding a used baking pan, neither had checked to discover how badly it had been used.

Maggie, ever ready to overcome adversity, hustled to Adams, our local bakery, arriving just before they closed. She bought a magnificent chocolate cake and delivered it to the bake sale collection point – where it drew "oohs" and "ahs."

Thankfully she did not enter the lottery and win it back. She would have won.

# The Thinking Couple's Guide to Managing Money

Money, like sex, is a couples' subject now.

There is an old saying that "money can't buy happiness." That's a half-truth. Money, or, more accurately, the failure to deal with money issues can buy you a lot of unhappiness in marriage. That's why money, like sex, is a subject that demands mutual understanding and exploration.

You see it's all about you—young women with a new sense of self-worth, better educated with better skills. You see women working not only for economic necessity but for career satisfaction and personal growth. And you see women making an important financial contribution toward a couple's present living standard and future goals.

Nonworking women too find that involvement with money matters is part of their lives, especially through new laws that provide that part of a husband's individual retirement account may be put under a wife's name, that Social Security payments now cover a wife for life after ten years of marriage, that credit information histories on joint charge accounts must now be reported in the name of each spouse.

As this trend continues, mutual participation in money matters may not only be the hallmark of a thinking couple—it may also be a form of "marriage insurance."

—From "The Thinking Couple's Guide to Managing Money," by Maggie Tripp and Gonnie Siegel, *Modern Bride* magazine, March 1979

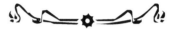

# Business School Case History

To say Maggie was a restless person would be to understate and oversimplify.

She simply could not tolerate doing nothing. Doing something exciting—especially something no one had done before—was deeply embedded in her DNA.

Shortly after she had delivered our second child, Maggie cast about for a business that she could operate from the small desk that served as her home office. Instinctively, she followed a primary rule from Marketing 101: "Find a need and fill it."

Maggie observed a local niche market. Most women loved flowers in their homes, but that desire was frustrated by two things: flowers were expensive, and usually required a special trip to a florist.

Teaming up with a friend and neighbor named Doris Beifield, Maggie investigated the distribution chain of the floral industry. She found that it was, indeed, a mom-and-pop business. Flowers were raised in greenhouses by mostly independent entrepreneurs and shipped weekly into wholesale markets where the owners of local flower shops purchased limited inventories every week.

The retailers faced a very difficult and ongoing problem. Which flowers should they choose? Which flowers would sell that particular week? What to do with the flowers that wilted? The answer, of course, was to limit their inventory and to hope for orders for weddings, funerals, and such—events for which they could charge substantially more money. And of course florists long for opportunities to decorate big dinner parties.

The first breakthrough for Maggie and Doris came with the realization that they had to take the waste out of the distribution process. In addition, they had to attack the high cost of flowers.

In a brilliant insight, the two women almost simultaneously decided they could transfer the decision as to which flowers to buy each week from the consumer to themselves. If this would work, they could go to the flower market each week and choose those flowers that were most plentiful and least costly. They could even make an offer to the wholesaler to buy his whole inventory of any given flower at a very low price.

This left only the small problem of how to dispose of a large quantity of "any given flower." They discarded a number of avenues, including selling the flowers as "blankets" or commercial wall decorations or fundraisers for a charity.

Then Maggie said, "I think lots of people would like to have fresh flowers in their home every weekend. You know, we could deliver any flower we choose if people agreed to take them every week for a period of time. We could call it Flowers Every Friday. And if our price was cheap enough, I think people would accept whatever flower we chose."

That business plan worked. A small mailing to people in the local area created a nucleus of customers, and word of mouth did the rest. Each week about five a.m. Maggie and Doris rose, left their sleeping spouses, and drove down to the wholesale flower market. There they negotiated ever-larger orders of beautiful flowers, sometimes with a bit of greenery added for good measure. Then—Maggie in her Jeep and Doris in her wagon—off they went on delivery routes that covered several hundred customers before noontime.

With a cost averaging about one dollar per bunch of flowers and a selling price of four (later, five) dollars, with no store and no rent, what could go wrong?

The answer: success and weather. Success was a problem when the number of customers outran their capacity to deliver, and when hiring drivers turned out to be far more difficult than they had imagined. Weather was a problem when, in the midst of a gigantic snowstorm, Maggie called me at my office and said she didn't think she could drive the Jeep from City Line Avenue to our home in Mount Airy, a distance of only three miles. But she had a plan. She would leave the Jeep exactly where it was and walk a quarter mile to the Presidential Apartments where her aunt lived.

Maggie didn't get home until the next morning. The storm had shut down the city. And soon Maggie and Doris shut down the business.

# Instant Fame

**Sometimes** when Maggie had a speech to deliver, she recruited me as her factotum. Such was the case when Program Corporation of America booked her to address the International Federation of Teachers at their 1980 convention in Ottawa, Canada.

It was July, and we were taking a break at our home at Long Lake in Maine, opening an opportunity to drive to Ottawa by cruising along the US-Canadian border through the Black Forest-like woods of Vermont.

For some months, Maggie had been assembling the perfect talk for this sophisticated group. She called it "Portrait of a New Woman: The Fine Art of Change." It was, as you might surmise, an illustrated review of women artists over the centuries, delineating how extraordinary female artists produced some great art despite being denied both education and exposure. I had the honor of running the slide projector.

As we entered the lobby of the Chateau Laurier, a landmark hotel in Ottawa, a sign on an easel caught Maggie's eye: Yousuf Karsh, Portrait Photographer.

"I know who he is," she said. "You go get checked in. I'll find you."

Into Karsh's office she marched, where she told an uninterested young woman sitting at the reception desk, "I want to see Mr. Karsh."

The prompt response was that Mr. Karsh saw people only by appointment.

"You tell Mr. Karsh that my name is Maggie Tripp. I am the keynote speaker at the teachers convention today, I'm going back to Maine tomorrow, and I would like to do business with him today."

In a few minutes, Yousuf Karsh emerged from the studio door and asked graciously, "What can I do for you?"

Maggie explained that her husband had accompanied her from New York and Maine and that he had done so much work on her speech and the pictures of women's art and that she wanted to do something nice in return and that she had heard that Mr. Karsh was a wonderful talent and would he do her husband's portrait?

When she drew a breath, Karsh said, "Do you know how much I charge?"

"No," Maggie said, "but I'm the principal speaker here today, and I'll give you my entire fee if you'll do my husband's portrait."

Karsh didn't hesitate. "That's really wonderful. I'll be pleased to do it."

And that's how—for $2,500, since you're dying to know—I had my portrait taken by the man who had, from time to time, done portraits of Winston Churchill, Franklin D. Roosevelt, Fidel Castro, Humphrey Bogart, Ernest Hemingway, George Bernard Shaw, Pope John Paul II, Grace Kelly, and Albert Einstein.

And that's how I came to mingle with the rich and the famous.

If "the free married woman" sounds like a contradiction in terms, let me explain: I am describing a woman who is not only part of a couple but also a fully realized, independent person. She is secure economically because she has a skill. She is secure emotionally because her role in the combination is not simply supportiveness and self-sacrifice but also active direction and tangible contributions.

She affects their style of living on many levels: their political activity and community participation, where they live, when and if they have children. She is free to develop her own self within the framework of the relationship. What a marriage contract does, written or verbal, is to bring the issues out for an airing before they become problems.

—From the speech "Men and Women Face the Future— Together or Separately"
The University of Wisconsin
Madison, Wisconsin, October 1979

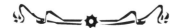

# That Championship Season—Part 1

**Way,** way back in 1949, the Philadelphia Eagles actually won the National Football League championship. Meanwhile, out in the far reaches of California, the Los Angeles Rams, then of the American Football League, won in their own trophy.

Naturally, a championship game between the two teams was needed to give the American people a true championship season. There were a few obstacles: like three thousand miles from coast to coast and no coast-to-coast cable TV connection.

Maggie's father, then one of a group of "brothers" who owned the Philadelphia Eagles, got me an introduction to Bert Bell, commissioner of the NFL. At that point I was running an ad agency, and with ineffable charm and certainty, I assured Mr. Bell I could arrange national television coverage of this great game. He granted me the TV rights.

When I told Maggie about the proposed groundbreaking television event, she said reassuringly, "You're absolutely crazy, dear, but why not?"

Friends of mine at WFIL-TV, the ABC outlet in Philadelphia, introduced me to network sports packagers who agreed to carry the event on their stations from Chicago eastward. There was, of course, no cable connection between Chicago and the West Coast! The ABC folks also informed me that they could not furnish any cameras or cameramen. The ABC network would pick up a feed in Chicago and send it zooming through the eastern cities, but that was all.

I recruited a camera crew consisting of Carl Volker and Ralph Lopatin, the news crew from the NBC station, and between us we conceived a plan to shoot the game at the Coliseum in Los Angeles, develop and edit the film on the chartered plane coming back to Chicago, and put it on the eastern ABC network as though it were live.

Meanwhile, the gods who were programming this unprecedented event were hard at work. The owners of the Eagles had arranged to bring the Super Chief—that gorgeous streamliner that ran from Chicago to Los Angeles—into Philadelphia specifically to transport the Eagles team, the press, and all related personnel directly from downtown Philadelphia to sunny LA. Maggie was delighted. She turned the television project into her personal exploration of the West Coast, exchanging our return tickets to route us through San Francisco, where she and her mother had arranged parties and tours.

All went well on the train trip to Los Angeles. I played bridge in the observation car with the Eagles' famed coach, Greasy Neale, who, it turned out, could remember all fifty-two cards in the order they were played. Maggie met many of the players, including Chuck Bednarik, probably the finest linebacker of all time, who succeeded in passing our roomette door at the exact same time Maggie emerged. Chuck was about twice as tall and four times as wide as Maggie—so the encounter became a question of physical agility. Maggie loved it.

We were greeted at the station by movie stars and a brass band. The California sun shined brightly—and we should have been suspicious. Having been transported to the Bel Air Hotel, having dispatched the camera crews and our announcer, Frank Reagan, to check out the stadium arrangements, Maggie and I settled in to enjoy the surroundings and get a good night's sleep.

The next morning we woke to an absolute downpour of rain. I immediately checked the weather forecast and learned that it was scheduled to rain for three days, including the day of the game!

Maggie took it all in stride. She arranged for a car to transport her to the leading department stores and to meet with childhood friends now living in Los Angeles. She also made it clear that, should it rain as advertised for the big game, she had no intention of sitting in a totally open stadium. She felt she had met enough of the Eagles team during the cross-country trip.

# That Championship Season—Part 2

The morning of the Rams-Eagles game dawned precisely as predicted. The rain gods generously poured buckets upon the ancient Coliseum in Los Angeles, the 110,000-seat stadium built for the Olympic games of 1920. Only 27,980 hardy fans showed up.

The best available shelter was in the press boxes that were located at the very top of the stadium—which is to say a quarter-mile from the playing field. However, there was a running track surrounding the football field, and the NFL officials agreed that the buses carrying dyed-in-the-wool football fans might drive onto this running track so the passengers could observe the game from the shelter of the buses.

Our camera crew, safely tucked into a small booth high above the stadium, filmed the entire game through telephoto lenses. The rain continued to descend, giving an artistic aura to the scene, a blessing because there was little resemblance to a standard football game. The players were slipping and sliding, and the ball was popping out of the hands of the most experienced quarterbacks. Not even the famed Steve Van Buren—Philadelphia's fabled running back, renowned for his ability to keep his feet in the face of vicious tackles—could stand up and gain yardage.

In the second quarter, the Eagles' great quarterback, Tommy Thompson fired a thirty-one-yard pass to Pete Pihos in the end zone. The score was now 7–0. Then, late in the third quarter, Los Angeles had the ball inside their own ten-yard line—and Philadelphia blocked a Rams punt. Defense man Leo Skladany felt the ball nestle in his arms and ran madly for the end zone. The Eagles could not score again, but the L.A. Rams, led by famous quarterback Bob Waterfield, were hapless. The game ended 14-–0.

Maggie enjoyed our return trip via San Francisco, where people loved her story of how she skipped the championship game and avoided pneumonia by staying out of the rain.

## Don't Leave It up to the Gypsies

My favorite "take charge" woman from the past is Annie Peck. She came from an austere New England family. Annie's older brothers shut her out of their athletic games … and Annie was jealous. So she devised her own program to strengthen herself physically.

Soon, Annie Peck became a great mountain climber. She conquered the Matterhorn. She climbed Mount Shasta in California. But what endears her to me is this: when Annie reached the peak of Mount Coropuna in

Peru—21,250 feet above sea level—she planted a pole with a banner that read VOTES FOR WOMEN!

—From the lecture "Don't Leave It up to the Gypsies!"
St. Norbert's College
DePere, Wisconsin, January 1977

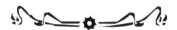

# Stop, Thief!

To have your car snatched from you is an unhappy, even shocking experience. Maggie managed to live through it not once but twice.

We had just returned from a trip to California, arriving that morning with our eyes appropriately red. I went to town to the office while Maggie went to our house in Rydal with eight-year-old daughter, Barbara. Our son, Jeff, was in school.

Maggie lay down and promptly dozed off, so when a knock came, Barbara swung open the big front wooden door. There stood a good looking man, well dressed in a sport coat, shirt, and tie.

"Give me the keys to the car," he said.

Barbara, confused, asked, "Why?"

The man repeated, "Just give me the car keys. Now!"

"I don't know where they are."

"Then go get your mother!"

When Maggie came to the scene, she noticed at once that the man had one hand wrapped in a handkerchief with blood seeping through. *Hmm … well spoken, well dressed … probably someone's houseman who got into a fight.*

She quickly decided he meant business and said, "Just a minute, I'll get the keys."

As she slipped into the kitchen and plucked the keys off their hook, she remembered something.

"Just another minute," she told the man. "My husband's camera equipment is in the trunk. We just got back from a trip, and he'll be really angry if I let his pictures go."

The man stood by while Maggie removed the camera cases from the trunk and then got in the driver's seat and zoomed out of the driveway. Maggie called the police.

When the police—and later the FBI—arrived, it turned out the man was Earl "Kill" Smith and that he had arrived at our door by scampering across the country, escaping from a botched robbery of the nearby Abington Bank. He was, the cops informed us, a dangerous criminal on the FBI's Ten Most Wanted list.

The FBI men questioned Maggie closely, implying she might have helped Earl "Kill" Smith escape, doubting anyone could have ordered this hardened criminal to stand by quietly while she rescued her husband's cameras from the trunk of their car.

Maggie convinced the FBI man that she was, indeed, innocent.

A year and a half later, Earl "Kill" Smith was captured, along with three co-workers, as they sped along the highway between Washington and Baltimore, having just stolen the payroll at Andrews Air Force Base. The loot, $112,000, was found in the trunk of that car. Smith died in a federal prison a few years later.

Maggie had one other car disappear. We were living in New York at the United Nations Plaza Apartments, from which I could walk to work daily, leaving our BMW in the garage, safely stored for weekend ventures.

On one fateful Saturday, we took the car down to Greenwich Village, where we enjoyed cocktails and finger food and a group of great people from the Village's abundance of artists and writers.

When we left to go home, we could not find the BMW. Did we forget where we parked it? Check the next block. No, it must be back where we looked the first time. No, it wasn't. Panic time. Call the cops!

Alas, the cops knew exactly what had happened. Our car had been towed away because it was on the list of people who had ignored too many parking tickets. Scofflaws? Not me!

Maggie quickly confessed. She had been using the car instead of public transportation or taxis. And yes, she had received occasional tickets, but they didn't matter—because, after all, the car was licensed in Maine!

It may have been licensed in Maine, but it was in the possession of New York City. Some $650 later—only cash accepted, thank you—paid to a grim-faced woman in an iron-barred cashier's cage, we rescued our BMW from a desolate lot in Brooklyn.

It was, I knew, fruitless to remonstrate with Maggie, but I did open the door: "Well, what do you think?"

Without blinking an eye, she answered: "I saved a lot of cab fares, didn't I? And think of all the times I *didn't* get a ticket."

# Department of Public Embarrassment

For all of her forceful character and quick response time, Maggie's efforts to restrain her mother's blunt public statements often ended not merely in failure but in embarrassment.

During our years in New York, Maggie made an earnest "good daughter" effort to get back to Philadelphia to see her mom. At one point, she persuaded Temple University to hire her to present a class on women controlling their own lives. Each week she took the train to Philadelphia, where she would present an hour and a half of lecture and debate on various aspects of women's independence.

As part of Maggie's professional engagement, she was allowed to invite her mother to audit the classes. After the presentation, Maggie and her mom would adjourn to the Warwick Hotel for lunch and chat. On the day of this particular scene, a woman named Jean came up to Maggie after class and earnestly begged for time to talk about her husband's attitude and their pending divorce. Maggie explained that she always lunched with her mother, Helen, before returning to New York.

She told Jean she would listen to her but her mother would have to be with them.

"No problem," Jean said.

After explaining the situation to her mother, Maggie took Jean and Helen to the Warwick for lunch. In an aside, Helen agreed that she would sit silently and not interfere with Maggie's counseling.

Jean's story was, indeed, heart-wrenching, though not extraordinary. After some twenty-six years of marriage, with two grown children now flown away, Jean's husband had told her that she was no longer attractive to him. In fact, he was quite frank and let her know who the other woman was: one of their close "friends." Jean had no work experience, but her husband was providing ample money—at least for the immediate future. What was she to do with the rest of her life?

Without hesitation, Maggie advised Jean to take inventory of her skills and inclinations, her talents and hobbies, and prepare herself for a useful life.

"When should I start dating?" Jean asked.

"Forget about men for now!" Maggie said incisively. "This is the time when you're most likely to make another big mistake. If there's anything you need right now, it's not just a replacement for that husband of yours."

At this point, Helen could no longer contain herself: "Don't listen to her, Jean! She's got Cary Grant at home!"

Maggie hissed, "Mother!" But it was too late.

Mother sat there with her arms crossed and her mouth closed. Maggie could manage everyone else in the world, but, once again, she had met her match in her mother.

# The Hand that Rocks the Cradle

For this symposium on personal finance for women, I can sum up my sentiments in a simple statement: "The hand that rocks the cradle should also count the cash. If you don't watch the money, who will?" Just remember Ralph Waldo Emerson's words: "Money is as beautiful as roses."

The future looks bright for women who keep a hand on their financial future. It used to be that the only thing a woman knew about money was how to manipulate her man to get it. Traditionally, girls have been brought up to marry millionaires while their brothers were told to grow up to become millionaires.

The reality is that 85 percent of adult American women will find themselves single, divorced, or widowed at some point, so it's common sense to know how to get a loan, apply for a credit card, and make other financial decisions. Making money work is woman's work now, and here's why: money buys what every woman wants–the freedom to take charge of her own life.

Believe me, knowing how to invest in the stock market can do more for a woman than greeting her man at the front door dressed in clear plastic wrap–especially as time goes by.

All this is not really new. Way back in 1877, Susan B. Anthony told her fellow feminists: "Don't let the years slip by without getting rich."

So when I tell you, a hundred years later, that the hand that rocks the cradle should also count the cash, it may not be new—but today it's actually possible.

—From the keynote speech
Mt. Holyoke College
April 1978

# Getting Exercised

Never one to do things by halves, Maggie was a vocal advocate for exercise. But how could she not be? Both her father and mother, each in their own peculiar ways, believed in exercise long before it became widely popular.

Her father, Jack Beresin, believed in a long daily walk. Monday through Friday he could be seen strutting vigorously from his apartment at Forty-Seventh and Pine streets to his office at Broad and Pine, a distance of almost two miles.

Of course Jack had a car and chauffeur, but he used this luxury only as an accessory to his exercise plan. He instructed the chauffeur to show up at his apartment each weekday at eight a.m. and then follow him with the car as he walked briskly to the office. That had a double benefit: in case of rain or snow, the ever-ready car provided immediate shelter, and if a friend should come along and offer him a ride, Jack would always point to his car and chauffeur and say, "No thanks. I can afford a car, but I can't afford to miss my daily walk."

Maggie's mother, Helen, on the other hand, considered walking an inconvenience. She believed she had enough exercise simply taking care of the children and the house. But she would not let anything deprive her of that activity.

For many, many years, the Beresins had a housekeeper named Amy, a corpulent woman who adored Maggie and her sister, knew exactly where everything was in the house, and would do anything in the world for "Miz. Beresin." But Helen didn't always let her.

As Maggie described, "It was normal that I'd come home from school and find Amy sitting on the couch in the living room while my mother ran around the room with the vacuum cleaner or dusted the furniture."

When Maggie pointed out to Helen that Amy was growing broader every day and needed the exercise, Helen responded, "She can take care of her figure by eating less. I can't just sit around the house all day—I need this exercise."

Maggie was an avid participant in yoga, bike riding, swimming, and any gym equipment she could get close to. We rode bicycles through the streets of New York and circled Central Park. She brought a yoga instructor to our New York apartment and graciously included me in the private instruction. We belonged to the health club high atop the United Nations Plaza Hotel where we could swim, play tennis, or work out separately or together.

It was there Maggie had one of her delightful adventures.

After a workout, she was sitting in the sauna when a young woman walked in—wearing nothing of course. Maggie quickly recognized her: it was Hana Mandlikova, the young woman we had seen the day before as she won the singles title at the United States Open tennis tournament.

Without hesitation, Maggie struck up a conversation with Hana, telling her how much she and I admired her courageous performance on the tennis court.

"Oh, thank you." Hana said. "And what do you do, Maggie?"

"Well, I'm a college professor and a writer. I especially deal with the subject of women."

"You're a writer? That's good. You know, Martina Navratilova has a book about how to play the game. I know as much as she does … but I don't know how to write. Do you think you could write a book for me? By the way, Maggie, do you play tennis?"

Maggie, in a flash of genius, responded unhesitatingly and quite truthfully: "Almost."

They left the subject there.

When Maggie got dressed, she rushed home to tell me about Hana Mandlikova's gorgeous body and how she must have trained to get it in that shape. I told her the next time she had such an encounter to just call me and I would gladly come over and pick her up at the health club.

# A Matter of Taste

By default, many adult women define their lives in terms of their children. When they talk with other women, children are the main topic—sometimes the only topic.

Maggie's children were important not merely from the standpoint of loving one's own offspring but as individuals, learning to stand on their own two feet. Applying her principles to two very different personalities was, however, a challenge.

Jeffrey, our firstborn, was a handsome, strong-willed, outgoing, determined boy, while Barbara, our second child, two years younger, was a lovely, soft-spoken, sensitive, and outwardly meek girl. Each required thoughtful upbringing.

One story epitomizes Maggie's best approach to child rearing. In 1960, we took the family to Paris as part of a European cultural indoctrination. Maggie had a great idea for art education. Instead of relying only on a visit to museums, the Louvre and such, she let the children visit art galleries and begin their own art collections. We would give the children $500 (real money then) each and let them buy their first painting. Jeff, then fifteen, cheered and seized the occasion to go off on his own to explore the art world of Paris. Barbara was only too happy to go with us to known galleries.

Maggie and Barbara and I set off for the 8th Arrondissement straight for the gallery where a good friend, Mona Kline, had bought several paintings by well-known artists. The mention of Mona's name brought forth the gallery owner—whom we shall call Monsieur because his name is buried in our archives—and we explained to him that it was our daughter who sought her first fine-art acquisition.

During our conversation, Barbara had been surveying the array of oils on the walls. When Monsieur asked her if she saw anything suitable, she pointed to a small gold-framed drawing and unhesitatingly replied, "Oh, yes, that one. I really love that. Who is the artist?"

"Well, my dear," Monsieur said, "you have good taste. That's a pencil drawing by a man named Camille Pissaro. He used that farm woman sowing seeds in his later oil paintings."

"I love it," Barbara repeated. "I really love it."

"About how much money did you want to spend for your first art?" Monsieur asked.

Proudly lifting her head, Barbara replied, "Oh, my parents gave me $500. I can spend it as I choose."

Monsieur gulped, turned slightly red, and said, "My dear, that Pissaro is yours."

Back at our hotel, Maggie and Barbara and I settled in, content with the good fortune of the day, awaiting Jeff's return from the streets of Paris. When he arrived, he made a grand entrance with a three-foot-high painting wrapped in brown paper, clutched in his arms.

"Where have you been?" Maggie asked.

"All over Paris, but mainly in Montmartre. That's where many artists hang out. And look what I found … and it was less than the $500."

With a wide sweep of his arm like a magician, Jeff slid the wrapping off the paper to reveal a portrait of a woman wearing a black dress standing against a dark background and holding before her a single white lily.

Barbara laughed softly, I bit my lip, and Maggie commanded, "You take that back in the morning! That's the most depressing thing I've ever seen. You can't start an art collection with that!"

"You said I could buy whatever I wanted!" he said. And so it went.

Barbara's Pissaro is now the treasured property of her daughter, Abby. The lady-with-a-lily eventually mysteriously disappeared, and Jeff and Maggie never discussed art again for many years.

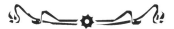

# Women Changing Society: An Irreversible Trend

And now the forecasts:

First, women will continue to move from being inner-oriented to being outer-oriented. They will have multiple life patterns. Some will blend work-life and family-life—some will do only one or the other—still others will work and then marry or live with someone and then go back to work. There will be no one way for all.

Second, our nation will benefit from having the best brains at work—not just the best male brains, but the best brains in the entire working population.

Third, I believe the American example will have global influence. It will be difficult to ignore.

Finally, I predict that—while we may never live in Candide's "best of all possible worlds"—the growing role of women may well be the key to a far better world than any we have seen until now.

—From "Women Changing Society: An Irreversible Trend" United States International Communications Agency Paris, France, November 1978

# Do You Love Me?

As these snapshots of Maggie have revealed, we were two totally different personalities, two opposite personas, people who might have clashed as easily as clung. I was more the romantic, she the didactic.

Nowhere was this more crisply illustrated than in her response to my frequent affirmation of affection: "You know I love you."

"Umm-hmm," she would reply.

"I do. I really love you."

"Yes, right."

"Maggie, do you love me?"

With her disingenuous, deadpan look, she would invariably say, "I'm thinking about it."

Two months before she left me forever, on our seventy-third anniversary, Maggie—at long last--changed her response:

"I think you could say that."

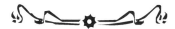

## And the Final Words Are Her Own

The woman who is both free and married loves in a special way: her love permeates but does not smother. Because of her ability to grow and change, she is the toughest competition against the attractions of other women.

The American male has always thought of himself as free…until he was married. The new American woman is about to show him that freedom is indivisible, that a marriage in which both partners are free and un-dependent is the only kind you can live with over time.

—From *The Free Married Woman*
Arbor House, 1974

Printed in the United States
By Bookmasters